> GLOBAL ISSUES

GLOBALISATION

Harriet McGregor

WAYLAND

First published in 2008 by Wayland

Copyright © Wayland 2008

Wayland
338 Euston Road
London NW1 3BH

Wayland Australia
Level 17/207 Kent Street
Sydney NSW 2000

Senior Editor: Claire Shanahan
Designer: Phipps Design
Photo Researcher: Louise Edgeworth
Proofreader and Indexer: Jo Kemp

British Library Cataloguing in Publication Data
McGregor, Harriet
Globalisation. - (Global issues)
1. Globalisation - Juvenile literature
I. Title   303.4'82

ISBN 978 0 7502 5437 3

Alamy: Carol & Mike Werner p17, Simon Rawles p30; Associated Press: Abe
Fox p12; Camera Press, London: Herzau/Laif p18, Hoehn/Laif p25; Corbis
Images: Lester Lefkowitz p6 and cover, Bettmann p10, Liba Taylor p20, Louisa
Gouliamaki/epa p33; Getty Images: Stone+/Base p5, Hulton Archive p8, Time
& Life Pictures p9, Hulton Archive p11, AFP p24, Pete Oxford/Minden Pictures
p26, Karen Kasmauski/Science Faction p34, Yu Mizuno/Ailead/Amana Images
p40 and cover; Panos Pictures: Mark Henley p15; Reuters: Jean-Philippe Arles
p16, Andy Clark p36, Keith Bedford p41, Bobby Yip p42, Claro Cortes p44,
Feisal Omar p45; Rex Features: Sipa Press p21, p22, Image Source p28, p38.

Printed in China

Wayland is a division of Hachette Children's Books,
an Hachette Livre UK company.
www.hachettelivre.co.uk

Contents

Chapter 1

What is Globalisation?

Today, we hear people talk about globalisation on television and radio, and we read about it in books and newspapers. What is globalisation?

Globalisation is the way in which our world has become more integrated, or joined-up. People, governments and countries are more dependent on each other today than they were in the past.

> QUOTE >
>
> 'Globalization is a force that increasingly touches the lives of people living in all countries of the world.'
>
> IMF website, 2007.

Hundreds of years ago, people lived very isolated lives, often not moving far from where they were born. They did not have cars, trains or aeroplanes. Without telephones, email and the Internet, they were out of touch with most others in their country, let alone people on the far side of the planet. From the 19th century onward, new transport and communications technologies transformed this situation.

Trade and globalisation

International trade (buying and selling) of goods, services and currency is enormous and continuous in the present day. But why do countries trade with each other? Individual countries can be particularly good, or bad, at growing certain crops or producing certain goods and services. For example, rice grows abundantly in flooded fields in tropical countries with warm, damp climates, such as are found in some south-east Asian countries. Rice would not grow as well in cold, dry climates. Other countries may have different resources, such as an educated workforce or rich natural resources, like copper or iron. People use their resources in order to produce and trade goods or services and, importantly, to make a profit.

Many everyday goods that we take for granted are global goods – they are made in more than one country. A mobile phone, for example, could have a battery made using cobalt from a mine in the Democratic Republic of Congo in Africa, which is processed by a Belgian-run factory. The microchip could have been designed by Indian engineers and produced in Taiwan. The phone may have been conceived in Finland, assembled in Hungary, and finally sold in your home town.

Now, there are also fewer barriers to trade between nations than there have been in the past. Goods, services and capital (money) move easily between

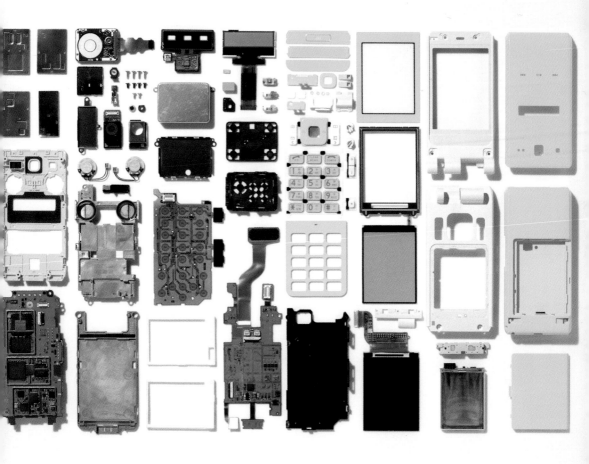

countries, feeding globalisation. Corporations compete with one another to sell their products to as many people as possible, and in doing so become extremely wealthy and powerful (see pages 18–19). As corporations have expanded and begun to trade internationally, they are able to make use of their economies of scale. This means that the larger a company becomes and the more it produces, the cheaper it can produce each unit of its product (see pages 14–15). One reason for this is that

Making an everyday product is often a global operation. Mobile phones are composed of many different substances or components, which are sourced or produced in a variety of locations across the world.

larger companies often have greater purchasing powers. They can receive discounts for placing huge orders for raw materials or components for their product. As a result, the cost of each item is lower, meaning greater profits for the company and cheaper products for the consumer.

Work, communication and globalisation

Travel and communication are easier and cheaper in the 21st century than they have ever been. The invention of the Internet allows instant communication across thousands of kilometres. Air travel has made the world a smaller place and many people now work and live away from their home countries. Companies spread their offices all over the world. They may move

In almost any city worldwide, billboards and neon signs advertise products and services, like these in New York, in the United States of America.

to where labour is cheap or where raw materials are in plentiful supply (see pages 26–27). English has become the dominant language in business, particularly on the Internet. As a result, societies everywhere affect each other and rely on each other in countless ways, accelerating globalisation.

 Until the 1830s The fastest way to send a long-distance message is to use a carrier pigeon >>> | **1960s** The word 'globalisation' first comes into use >>> | **1980s** and **1990s** Globalisation takes off with force >>>

Culture and globalisation

It is not only finance, trade and travel that are affected by globalisation. Each one of us and our culture is also influenced. A 'culture' is a set of beliefs, attitudes and practices shared by a group of people. Cultures are affected by the people that belong to them as well as by outside influences. These influences include what you see on television, the products that you buy, the food that you eat, and the things you read about in magazines, newspapers, books and on the Internet.

Westernised culture means the set of attitudes, beliefs and practices shared by people living in the United Kingdom (UK), the United States of America (USA), Western Europe and other more economically developed countries (MEDCs). Many people feel that globalisation is spreading Westernised culture around the world. Companies like McDonald's, Nike, Vodafone and Wal-Mart are everywhere, including in less economically developed countries (LEDCs).

Politics and globalisation

Politics are activities associated with governments. Governments consist of many departments, each responsible for a particular area of a country's activities, such as trade, transport, defence, health and education. In our globalised world, governments of different countries often need to work together. Global organisations have been set up to help this process (see pages 24–25).

> **QUOTE >**
>
> 'Telecommunications is creating a global audience. Transport is creating a global village. From Buenos Aires to Boston to Beijing, ordinary people are watching MTV, they're wearing Levi's jeans, and they're listening to Sony Walkmans as they commute to work.'
>
> 'Beyond Borders: Managing a World of Free Trade and Deep Interdependence', World Trade Organisation (WTO), 1996.

The international body G8 was set up in 1975 to discuss the economic problems of the day and is still functioning today. Representatives from (left to right) Japan, Canada, France, Russia, Germany, the USA, the UK and Italy, along with European Union President José Barroso, met in host country Germany in June 2007 for the annual summit.

From 1900 Music from Africa and Latin America begins influencing (and still does) Western music >>>

2007 Around three-quarters of the information on the Internet is in English >>>

Chapter 2

The History of Globalistion

Over thousands of years, much of the world's human population has been changing gradually from an isolated, self-sufficient existence, to a way of life that involves trade and increasing interaction with our international neighbours.

The ancient world

The first humans were hunters of animals and gatherers of plants for food. Around 8,000 BCE, people began to produce their own food by growing crops and keeping animals. The success of this led to food surpluses (extras), so trade in food began. Populations increased, villages and towns formed and, in time, city-states and nations developed. Trade continued to grow. Even so, little or no long-distance interaction took place until ancient peoples such as the Phoenicians began to take to the seas.

Growing skill in ship-building and navigation allowed increasingly long voyages, and the Greeks, the Romans and the Arabs formed long-distance trading links. With the fall of the Roman Empire, trade decreased, but as Europe passed from the Dark Ages to the Medieval period, there was increasing land-based contact with India and China.

Exploration and colonisation

By the time of Christopher Columbus (1451–1506), it was generally accepted that the Earth is spherical.

European explorers sailed west in search of what they hoped would be an uninterrupted sea-passage to the lands of the east. Instead, they reached coastal regions of the Americas, and colonisation began. European countries such as the Netherlands, Britain, France, Spain and Portugal began to take control of trade in parts of Africa, the Americas and Asia. Slavery of the natives became widespread.

At its height, the British Empire controlled a global population of more than 450 million people. These British colonials are in Secunderabad, near the city of Hyderabad in India.

In the 1800s, factories such as this one making bicycles sprang up across Britain. The mechanisation of industry gave a huge boost to globalisation.

The Industrial Revolution

In the late 1700s, the Industrial Revolution began in Britain and rapidly spread to other European countries. The economies of Britain and these other countries had been based on manual labour, but in the Industrial Revolution, the production of goods such as textiles became mechanised. Iron-making techniques were developed, roads were improved, canals were dug, and above all, the introduction of the railway drastically cut travel times. As a result of these developments, many new manufacturing processes rapidly developed, people were able to travel faster and further, trade grew enormously, and society changed forever.

Three new inventions spurred on further industrial development: electricity (first used in the mid-1800s), the internal combustion engine (invented in 1885) and telegraph communication across the Atlantic (set up in 1866). Telegraph communication led to the development of telephone communication and wireless radio.

QUOTE >

'We must find new lands from which we can easily obtain raw materials and at the same time exploit the cheap slave labour from the natives of the colonies. The colonies [will] also provide a dumping ground for the surplus goods produced in our factories.'

Cecil Rhodes, the founder of Rhodesia, now known as Zimbabwe, quoted in *The Ecologist*, 1890s.

Berlin in Germany was just one of the cities devastated by bombing during World War II. Here, twisted metal frames are visible through the walls of the buildings.

The impact of world war

Trade continued to grow between 1850 and 1914, but was then interrupted by World Wars I and II (1914–1918 and 1939–1945 respectively). Some trading countries underwent an economic depression and unemployment grew. Countries tried to protect their own industries and make sure their own people had jobs. To do this, they stopped the purchase of foreign goods.

After World War I (WWI), the League of Nations was formed to reduce the likelihood of war through the promotion of diplomacy and negotiation between nations. However, it failed to prevent World War II (WWII) and was superseded by the United Nations (UN) in 1945.

Bretton Woods Conference

In July 1944, representatives of 44 countries met in a town called Bretton Woods in the USA (see pages 12–13). This conference was the first attempt to create rules to govern the global economy. They wanted to make trade easier and improve the way capitalism operates. Capitalism is the system in which trade and industry are owned and run by private businesses for profit.

Out of the meeting, three institutions were created: the International Monetary Fund (IMF), the World Bank (originally the International Bank for Reconstruction and Development) and, a few years later, the General Agreement on Tariffs and Trade (GATT).

The IMF's goals were numerous. For instance, to create economic stability; to help international trade to grow; to increase employment and income; to make it easier to exchange one currency for another when trading across international borders; to give emergency loans to countries in need; to reduce trade barriers and tariffs. Tariffs are fees added to imports or exports. For example, if a government puts a tariff on imports of steel, it makes the steel expensive to buy in that country. So instead, people are encouraged to buy steel that is not imported. Tariffs are designed to protect a country's economy, but they also reduce international trade.

The World Bank's goal was to provide money to European countries devastated by war. This money was for infrastructure such as power plants, dams, roads, airports, ports and education systems.

The GATT's goals were to help remove barriers to trade and to set rules on global trade in industrial goods. In 1995, GATT was replaced by the World Trade Organisation (WTO). The WTO does not set rules on trade. Instead, it makes sure that trade agreements are followed, it settles trade disputes and it oversees new trade agreements between countries.

New housing in London was funded by the World Bank as part of the restoration of infrastructure in countries affected by WWII.

24 October 1929 Stock prices on the New York Stock Exchange collapse, signalling the start of the Great Depression in the USA >>>

3 September 1939 Outbreak of WWII >>>

Summer 1945 WWII ends after more than 50 million civilian and military deaths >>>

11

Case Study: The Bretton Woods Conference, 1944

The Bretton Woods Conference took place in July 1944. Around 700 people from 44 countries descended on the beautiful resort of Bretton Woods, in New Hampshire, USA. Their common goal was to avoid the closed markets and economic warfare of the 1930s.

For three weeks, delegates at the Bretton Woods Conference discussed monetary and trade policies designed to improve economic growth.

Two plans

Although 44 nations were represented, discussions were dominated by two plans – one from the mighty USA and one from the almost bankrupt Britain.

The British plan was to create a system that encouraged economic growth. British Lord Keynes wanted to create a world currency reserve that would be managed by a central bank. This bank would be able to create money. Overall, the plan meant that wealthy countries would import more goods from less wealthy countries in an attempt to balance world trade.

The US plan aimed to create price stability in the world's economies, for example by reducing inflation. The US did not take Keynes' plan seriously. This may have been because the US was very wealthy. Because the US was extremely powerful, it 'won' and the IMF was born (see pages 10–11).

Today's viewpoints

There are both supporters and critics of the Bretton Woods system today. Many see the benefits that it has bestowed upon the world – an increase in global trade, huge economic growth and the bailing out of countries in crisis. But there are just as many, if not more, who are very critical of the system. They feel that it has only benefited wealthy countries and corporations and has done nothing for the world's poor and the environment.

WHAT THE WORLD THINKS...

These are three articles from newspapers around the world commenting on the Bretton Woods Conference in 1944. Compare and contrast the various viewpoints and see if you can find any more newspaper reports or other media discussing the conference.

Zac Goldsmith,
The Observer website,
20 May 2001

'...The goals that were set 50 years ago remain unchanged and, in fact, have been achieved many times over. Since Bretton Woods, for instance, the world has seen a 12-fold increase in global trade and a five-fold increase in economic growth. But during that same period, the world has deteriorated. Nearly three billion people today survive on less than [US]$2 (£1.40) a day, per capita incomes are falling in 80 countries, and life expectancy has declined in 33 countries since 1990. Meanwhile, the global environment lies close to ruins.'

The New York Times,
18 July 1944

'The delegates at Bretton Woods – above all, the American delegates – seem to be obsessed by the idea of machinery. They act as if international economic cooperation could be achieved only by setting up some elaborate organization, with funds and quotas and votes and rules and whereases, and as if the mere existence of such machinery in itself constitutes a solution of the problem. In their determined efforts to secure agreement on the superficial problems of machinery they have failed to secure or even to seek agreement on the really basic problem of principles.'

China Daily website,
29 August 2006

'In the early 1990s, the fund [IMF] was involved in bailing out Mexico. Later in the decade it helped rescue Thailand, South Korea and several other Asian countries from insolvency...'

Chapter 3

The Causes of Globalisation

Trade has grown rapidly since the Bretton Woods conference. With the ending of the Cold War in 1991, the former communist countries entered the global trading system. Asian countries reduced their trade barriers and globalisation really took off.

Profit

Companies go global to increase profits. Profit is the money that is left over when all of the costs of making, marketing, distributing and selling a product are deducted. To increase profits, companies must sell to more people and make products more cheaply. One way to do this is to transfer their activities outside the company's country of origin. They may move to where labour is cheap, flexible and unregulated, to where taxes are very low or where there is very little environmental protection. These factors all help companies reduce costs and increase profits.

Competition

Most companies experience competition from other companies. Companies are in competition when two or more companies try to sell the same product or service to the same group of people. The consumer must choose which company to purchase from. Many factors influence the consumer's decision, including price, quality or how easy it is to obtain the product. A company can attract a consumer by offering a great deal, or it can move into a new market where there is little or no competition.

A market isn't just a set of stalls in a town square. It also means the region or country where a company sells its products. Markets can become saturated with a product, resulting in a great deal of competition. A company may struggle to go on selling its products. There are often new markets in other countries. By moving into new markets, often as a result of competition, companies cause globalisation.

Economies of scale

Once a company has invested a lot of time and effort in the creation of a product, it can then make more of the same product at a fraction of the cost. This is called taking advantage of the economies of scale. For example, the company may get bulk deals on raw materials from its suppliers. It can purchase large industrial machines to make the product. To make using the machine efficient, it must produce thousands of items. A company may choose to sell its large number of cheaply produced items internationally.

Sometimes a company is 'safer' if it sells its products to more than one market. If there is an economic crisis in one country, the company can still expect

to sell in the other countries in which it is based. Globalisation is caused because companies want to protect themselves by spreading their business as widely as possible in different markets in order to minimise risk.

Fast-food restaurants have expanded across the world. Although they sometimes alter some of their products to suit a particular market, the overall look and feel of the brand is very much the same. Here, you can see the recognisable branding of KFC in just one branch of the chicken chain's 11,000-plus outlets in more than 80 countries.

Developments in technology

Since 1980, technology has caused globalisation to take off in a big way. Powerful computers allow companies to operate in many different currencies. Fibre optic cables and satellites transmit telephone calls and digital information instantly. Companies can work more easily with suppliers, manufacturers and sales teams all over the world.

Transportation technology has also improved and goods can be more easily transported by air and sea. World air cargo traffic tripled between 1985 and 1997 and is predicted to triple again by 2015. In 2005, American exporters spent US$3 billion less to ship their goods to market than they did in 1985. Rates on the three main US shipping routes fell

Despite rising fuel prices, air travel continues to grow rapidly, with companies producing larger and faster aeroplanes.

between 23 and 46 per cent.

As a result of the ease with which goods and people can be transported, companies do not always need to be near their plants and factories or near their target markets (where they want to sell their goods). They can go wherever is cheapest. This has helped to cause globalisation.

Geography

Because our planet revolves every 24 hours, the Sun rises and sets at different times all over the world. For example, sunrise in India happens five and a half hours before sunrise in the UK. If a company spreads out to several different time zones, it can continue to work around the clock without paying the extra wages usually required for night shifts.

The variety of climate and availability of natural resources on Earth is another cause of globalisation. Some companies relocate

1961 The first silicon microchip is invented >>> | Between 1995 and 2005 There is a 74 per cent rise in the amount of freight carried by the world's airlines >>> | By 2007 At any one time, there are between 8,000 and 18,000 aeroplanes in the skies around the world >>>

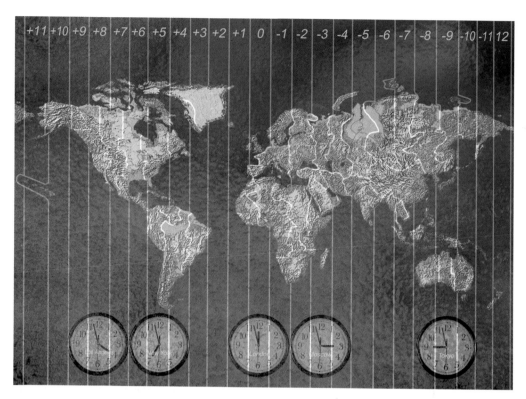

This map shows the world's time zones. If you had to situate a company in two countries, which two would you choose to make the most of the time differences?

to be near natural resources, such as coal, precious stones or metal ores (rocks containing metals), or they may move to areas that are particularly good for growing certain crops or foodstuffs, such as soy beans, oranges or grapes. This reduces the expense of transporting heavy or perishable goods.

Media and cultural changes

Today's media includes television, newspapers, magazines, the Internet, film, radio and other music sources, books and computer games. The media is our main source of information about the world. Through the media and the advertising it provides, people see and desire goods and lifestyles from different countries. Some say that, because of this, our tastes are converging (becoming more similar), which makes it easier for a company to sell the same product in many countries. (It is also more efficient for a company to sell lots of the same product, rather than a variety of products.) There aren't many countries where it is impossible to buy a Big Mac or a can of Coca-Cola. The media has helped to create a world market and cause globalisation.

2007 McDonald's has 30,000 restaurants worldwide and serves 52 million customers every day >>>

Case Study: Wal-Mart, the global retail giant

Wal-Mart has grown from just one store in 1962 in Arkansas, USA, to nearly 7,000 stores worldwide today. Wal-Mart attributes its success to two main things – an understanding of what the customer wants and the implementation of a computer system to track sales and inventory.

Going global

By 1990, Wal-Mart had saturated the American market and was soon to have stores in 50 states. To continue to increase profits, it was time to go global. The first international store was built in Mexico in 1991. Initially, Wal-Mart did not take into account differences between the Mexican and American cultures, trying to sell products such as ice skates and leaf blowers. When Wal-Mart adapted to the local environment, the store took off.

Domination

Today, Wal-Mart has stores in 14 countries. It has incredible global buying power because it is able to order huge amounts of stock at reduced prices. It can therefore sell its products at discounted prices – something that an existing local store will struggle to do.

Workers' rights

Wal-Mart has been much criticised in the media for its dislike of unions, but in contrast has been named 'America's most admired company' in *Fortune* magazine. The difference in opinion depends on how you measure a company's success – by economics or by the way in which some claim that it treats workers. For example, there have been reports of illegally long hours and violence in one Chinese factory that made handbags sold in Wal-Mart. Wal-Mart hires auditors to check conditions in factories that make its products, but situations like this one suggest that the system may not be 100 per cent fail-safe.

This huge Wal-Mart superstore in Dortmund, Germany, has been sold since the company was ordered to stop undercutting local shops.

 2000 Wal-Mart is accused of selling goods at prices so low that they are intentionally designed to drive other companies out of business >>>

2003 Wal-mart is ordered by the High Court in Germany to raise its prices because it is undermining the local competition >>>

WHAT THE WORLD THINKS...

These are three articles from newspapers around the world commenting on the Wal-Mart empire. Compare and contrast the various viewpoints and see if you can find any more newspaper reports or other media discussing the store.

Abir Pal,
The Times Of India
website,
28 Nov 2006

'From underpaying workers, squeezing suppliers to monopolistic practices and wiping out neighbourhood mom-and-pop stores, [Wal-Mart] has been accused of all these, in its endeavour to sell at the lowest price.'

Business Wire,
23 February 2004

'FORTUNE announced today that Wal-Mart is No. 1 on the magazine's annual list of America's Most Admired Companies.'

The New York Times website,
9 January 2006

'Wal-Mart has long been known for its bare-knuckled approach to fighting unions. When employees at an outlet in Canada voted last year to unionize, the retailer shut the store down, arguing it was unprofitable. In 2000, shortly after 11 Wal-Mart meat cutters in Texas voted to form a union, the company eliminated meat-cutter jobs companywide and announced it would use prepackaged meat instead...'

2005 Labour unions create new organisations and websites to influence the public against Wal-Mart >>> | **2006** Wal-Mart's annual sales top US$345 billion >>> | **2007** Wal-Mart has 1.9 million employees worldwide and 180 million customers each week >>>

Chapter 4

The Impact of Globalisation

The impact of globalisation has not been evenly spread. While globalisation has increased trade and lifted many out of poverty, the standard of living in other parts of the world has suffered. For instance, Christian Aid says that, 'sub-Saharan Africa is a massive US$272 billion worse off because of 'free' trade policies forced on them as a condition of receiving aid and debt relief.'

Free trade

Since WWII, free trade has been encouraged. The idea behind free trade is that anyone should be allowed to trade with anyone else.

LEDCs

Free trade allows global companies to move into a country and compete with local companies. However, fledgling industries in LEDCs do not have the resources to compete with global companies. When today's global companies first formed, they did not have the same level of global competition as there is today, and they were protected by subsidies and tariffs. A subsidy is money given to a private company to help it function. For example, if a government gives money to a steel manufacturer, it can afford to sell its steel more cheaply. This protectionism helps the company to compete in the marketplace.

Today, LEDCs are encouraged to embrace free trade, but ironically, Europe and North America still subsidise their farmers with billions of dollars. It is very hard for farmers in LEDCs to export to these markets.

LEDCs can make certain gains, such as increased employment, an improvement in workers' skills and an increase in income tax.

MEDCs

Globalisation and free trade can mean more choice and cheaper prices for consumers in MEDCs, and more profit for global companies. However, to reduce costs, companies in MEDCs outsource their workforce. Companies employ workers in a country where labour prices are lower, such as India. This can cause a boost to the economy of the offshore country, but a loss of jobs in the MEDC.

Consumers benefit from free trade when it results in cheaper goods.

Global loans

In our global economy, loans are given by the IMF and the World Bank to help a LEDC develop. The LEDC must pay back the debt over a period of time with an additional payment called interest.

In return for an IMF loan, the country may have to make some changes to the way in which it operates. These changes are called structural adjustments. The aim is to improve the country's economy. However, many people argue that structural adjustments are unfair. The country may have to agree to privatise its services, end government subsidies or spend less on healthcare or education. LEDCs can become caught in a cycle where they can only just afford to pay back the debt and have little left over for basic services.

Structural adjustments can force governments to privatise healthcare in LEDCs, such as the health clinic shown here, in Merti in Kenya.

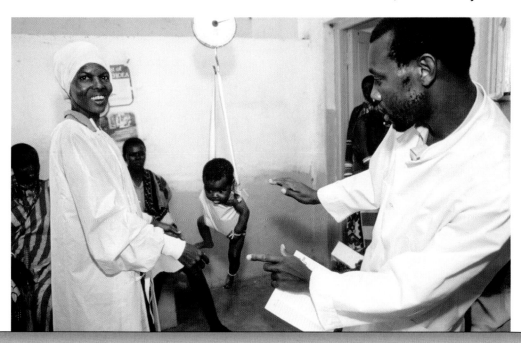

Climate change

The Earth is surrounded by a layer of gases called the atmosphere. The atmosphere lets through the Sun's rays. Carbon dioxide and other gases in the atmosphere trap some of these rays, and keep the Earth warm. This is the greenhouse effect.

When greenhouse gases are released into the atmosphere, they build up and trap even more heat. The subsequent warming of the earth is called global warming. If global warming continues for long enough, the weather conditions in an area may change over a period of time. This is climate change.

The Brazilian rainforest is being destroyed to create agricultural land and to harvest valuable timber.

We burn fossil fuels in cars, aeroplanes, factories, ships and power stations and this releases carbon dioxide and other greenhouse gases into the atmosphere. Over the last 30–50 years, the amount of carbon dioxide being emitted by burning fossil fuels has risen dramatically. Atmospheric carbon dioxide levels are at their highest for 450,000 years. As international trade and travel increases, so does the impact on our planet.

Resources

Globalisation is also using up natural resources fast and is producing massive amounts of waste and pollution. The oil, coal and gas that fuelled the Industrial Revolution is being used up. Oil will run

QUOTE >

'Rising demand for energy, food and raw materials by 2.5 billion Chinese and Indians is already having ripple effects worldwide…If China and India were to consume resources and produce pollution at the current US per capita level, it would require two planet earths just to sustain their two economies.'

Christopher Flavin and **Gary Gardner**, *State of the World*, 2006.

 Since 1860 19 of the 20 warmest years have occurred since 1981, and the five warmest since 1998 >>>

2006 A report from the IPCC states that the increase in globally average temperatures since the 1950s is more than 90% likely due to the observed increase in greenhouse gases >>>

QUOTE >

'Our village has been burning
forests to plant rice here for
generations. This is our way of life.
If we can't cut the forests, we can't
feed ourselves. The government
wants to protect the forests but
nobody cares about protecting the
peasants who live here.'

Dimanche Dimsay, chief elder of Mahatsara
Village, tells *BBC News*, 14 February 2005.

out within the next 40 years – within your lifetime. As we mine for minerals, destroy rainforests to grow crops and clear land for housing, factories and power plants, we wipe out habitats and wildlife and ruin delicately balanced ecosystems across the world. Some scientists believe that we are on the edge of a man-made mass extinction.

People who are opposed to globalisation believe that it encourages countries to exploit natural resources at unsustainable rates, especially in LEDCs where environmental regulation may not be as strict. Others argue the opposite. They say that the richer an economy becomes, the more likely it is to increase environmental controls and regulations.

In some parts of the world, people still depend on forests and other natural resources for their survival. They are often poor and, although they may be damaging the environment by, for example, cutting down trees, they often have no other option. Globalisation can result in new legislation that aims to protect the natural environment, but what about the people who rely on it?

Carbon footprint

The amount of carbon dioxide released by an individual, a company or country is called its carbon footprint. Carbon is released into the atmosphere by a huge variety of everyday activites, such as using a computer, switching on a light or travelling by car. Carbon is even released in the manufacture of your clothes, food and drink (see chart below). There is a lot of information in the media about reducing your carbon footprint.

This chart shows the main elements that make up the total of an average person's carbon footprint.

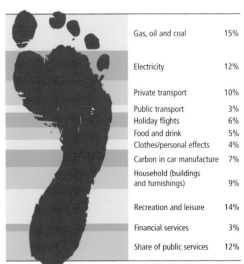

Gas, oil and coal	15%
Electricity	12%
Private transport	10%
Public transport	3%
Holiday flights	6%
Food and drink	5%
Clothes/personal effects	4%
Carbon in car manufacture	7%
Household (buildings and furnishings)	9%
Recreation and leisure	14%
Financial services	3%
Share of public services	12%

Source: www.carbonfootprint.com

 2008 Global temperatures are higher than they have been over the last 1,300 years >>>

Global politics

The political decisions that one country makes may affect another country. For example, one country may make a law that aims to reduce carbon emissions, but without the support of other countries, there will be no benefit to the environment. So, some decisions and laws have to be made on a global scale. Countries have grouped together and global organisations have been created to do this work, the most noteable being the United Nations (UN), formed in 1945.

Some political organisations are only open to countries in a certain region. 27 countries in Europe have grouped together to form the European Union (EU).

US President George W. Bush addresses the UN Security Council meeting on Africa in New York on 25 September 2007.

The African Union (AU) consists of 53 African states and the Association of South-East Asian Nations (ASEAN) consists of 10 countries in the south-east Asian region. These organisations make laws that affect their region of the world.

However, decisions made on a global scale cannot always benefit everyone. For example, the EU had promised to give preference to its former European colonies in Africa, the Caribbean and the Pacific, and to import bananas from these places. The USA argued with the EU because they said that it was unfair that they couldn't that they couldn't sell many bananas in the European markets. A WTO clause says that no-one is allowed to have a 'most favoured nation' and the WTO ruled in favour of the USA. By January 2006, the WTO had banned 'quotas' of bananas into the EU. Small banana-producing farmers in these nations are now at risk of losing their major export market.

Global community

Globalisation has led to an increased global citizenship. A citizen is someone who is a member of a community. Each of us is a member of the global community. There are many political organisations and treaties (formal contracts or agreements) that aim to keep members of the global community, and the planet itself safe.

For example, the International Criminal Court tries people who are accused of serious international crimes, such as genocide, war crimes and crimes against humanity. The UN addresses global political issues, such as international law, security, economic development and human rights issues.

Today, global citizens have an increasing awareness of what is happening in other parts of the world and what they can do to be an active member of the global community. The more we see and learn of other cultures, the more we may feel connected in a global social village.

Instant messaging and webcams make it easy to communicate with people all over the world. These advances in technology help us to feel part of a global community.

Case Study: Cargill, soy bean producer in the Amazon region

The Amazon rainforest covers more than 1 billion acres in South America, including parts of Brazil, Venezuela, Colombia, Ecuador and Peru.

The Amazon rainforest contains up to a fifth of the world's plant and animal species. It constantly recycles carbon dioxide into oxygen and helps regulate the Earth's climate.

The rainforest is being cut down for logging, cattle ranching and for growing crops for export. One of the main crops grown in the Amazon rainforest in Brazil is soy beans. Soy beans are shipped around the world to provide feed for chickens, which are sold to fast-food outlets and supermarkets.

Cargill

In 2003, American company Cargill opened up a large port on the Amazon River from which to transport soy beans, despite fierce opposition. That year, according to the Rainforest Action Network, $11,910^2$ kilometres of soy beans were planted and $18,000^2$ kilometres of rainforest were lost. Soy had become the greatest factor in the deforestation of the Amazon.

In March 2007, the port was shut down while the Brazilian government investigated whether Cargill had submitted the correct report to outline the impact of the port on the environment. The port opened up again just 20 days later and the case is ongoing.

Opinions

Cargill says that investment in the Santarém region and in Brazil as a whole is essential. The Brazilian government needs the soy bean industry, but says that it is also trying to protect the environment.

Some locals are cashing in on the new industry. Known as *grileiros*, they grab land wherever they can – usually illegally – and sell it to settlers wanting to grow soy.

Many of the local people want to protect their land, culture and environment, but they are threatened with violence. Those that protest against the loggers, soy producers and grileiros now fear for their lives.

1965 Cargill begins operating in Brazil >>>	Since 1995 Soy production in the Amazon has increased ten-fold >>>	1999 Work on the US$20 million port begins >>>	2003 The port opens >>>	By 2005 $26,000^2$ km of the Amazon has been cleared >>>

WHAT THE WORLD THINKS...

These are four articles from newspapers around the world commenting on the production of soy beans in the Amazon rainforest. Compare and contrast the various viewpoints and see if you can find any more newspaper reports or other media discussing the Cargill plant.

Associated Press, 26 March 2007

'Brazilian authorities have shut down an important deep water Amazon River soy export terminal owned by Cargill Incorporated. The shut-down came after a judge there ruled that the Minnesota-based agribusiness giant prepared an environmental impact statement that failed to meet Brazilian federal standards.'

Environment News Service, 29 March 2007

'It's important to remember that the Amazon…is one of the poorest regions in Brazil and the world, and there is a recognized need for responsible economic and social development. Economic development is the long-term solution to protecting both the Amazon's peoples and the environment…'

The Telegraph, 13 October 2007

'Many poor people lived on the land that the soya farmers wanted [when the Cargill grain terminal was built]. Some went voluntarily – selling off their plots – but some left under threats of violence. Communities disappeared and the landscape was razed.'

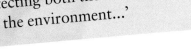

'Brazil, soy exporters in Greenpeace's sights', Tierramérica, 10 June 2006

'Laurance [an ecologist with the Smithsonian Tropical Research Institution, in Balboa, Panama] says huge foreign debt payments are driving this export of soybeans.'

The Tierramérica network is a collection of 26 newspapers published in Latin America.

> **March 2007** Port forced to shut, then re-opens illegally days later >>> | **2008** Every 24 hours, an area of Amazonian rainforest the size of 5,000 football pitches is burnt or chopped down >>> | **2008** Cargill believed to have plans to expand to the north of Santarém >>>

Chapter 5

Responses to Globalisation

The process of globalisation is embraced by some, but despised by others. Supporters of globalisation believe that increased trade, interaction and co-operation between nations can create a more equal, more peaceful and less narrow-minded world. They believe that globalisation will result in enhanced communities and greater understanding between cultures. The detailed arguments for globalisation are outlined below.

Trade and lifestyles

Globalisation supporters believe that an increase in trade results in an increase in wages, stimulates economic growth and creates jobs. Industrial capitalism has led to people in MEDCs living longer, healthier and more productive lives. The average life expectancy of someone living in the UK or USA is around 77 years, but it is between 40 and 55 years for someone living in sub-Saharan Africa. The hope is that in the future, the same benefits will come to those in LEDCs.

The environment

Supporters of globalisation say that when there is economic growth in a country,

In MEDCs, globalisation has resulted in wealth that is almost unimaginable for many people living in LEDCs.

there is an initial period during which the environment may suffer. But after this, there is a phase of improvement that begins when the per capita (per person) GDP reaches US$5000. GDP is the Gross Domestic Product of a country. It is a way of measuring the size of the economy. The greater the GDP, the better the economy.

Sweatshop workers

Globalisation is criticised for forcing people in LEDCs to work in 'sweatshops'. Sweatshops are factories where products such as clothing are made cheaply and the working conditions and pay are usually very poor. However, what is considered low pay in a MEDC is not necessarily low in a LEDC. In Vietnam, the growth of the footwear industry has led to a five-fold increase in wages of the employees. These wages would be considered a pittance in a MEDC, but in Vietnam it is enough to completely transform the lives of the workers for the better.

Consumers

Globalisation has led to lower prices and more choice for goods and services. In recent years, it has boosted the economies of two huge countries – China and India. In China, new investment has reduced the numbers of the extreme poor by half a billion people since 1990.

Globalisation itself is not the cause of poverty or of the widening gap between the rich and the poor. Instead, the world's poor remain so because of dictatorships, no protection of property rights, war, huge population growth, and economic policies imposed by goverments that destroy wealth rather than help to create it.

> **QUOTE >**
>
> 'Globalization is the process of integration of nations through the spread of ideas and the sharing of technological advances, through international trade, through the movement of labor and capital across national boundaries. It is a process that has been going almost throughout recorded history and that has conferred huge benefits. Globalization involves change, so it is often feared, even by those who end up gaining from it. And some do lose in the short run when things change. But globalization is like breathing: it is a not a process one can or should try to stop; of course, if there are obvious ways of breathing easier and better one should certainly do so.'
>
> **Anne O. Krueger**, First Deputy Managing Director of IMF, 2002.

Case Study: Fair Trade, the independent non-profit organisation

Fair Trade is a system in which farmers in LEDCs receive fair prices for their products, such as bananas, coffee and cocoa. Fair Trade allows farmers to trade globally while still maintaining a good standard of living.

Fair Trade across the globe

To be officially certified as 'Fair Trade', farmers have to be organised into co-operatives (democratically controlled groups). In order for farmers to be part of a Fair Trade co-operative and use a Fair

The Fair Trade logo is now a recognisable brand in itself, which is helping to raise sales of Fair Trade products by about 40 per cent per year.

Trade logo, they must stick to specific rules, which include using healthy and safe working conditions, equal opportunities and sustainable production techniques.

The Fair Trade price for a product is usually higher than the general market price. Many people, including Fair Trade farmers themselves, say that the farmers enjoy much improved lives when they receive a living wage for their product. To date, the Fair Trade system benefits more than 800,000 farmers in 48 countries.

A different system

Starbucks is the largest purchaser of Fair Trade coffee in the USA, but Starbucks actually prefers another system called the Coffee and Farming Equity practice (CAFE). This does not only give producers a fair price; it also helps provide finance, infrastructure and community development.

Is there another option?

Some suggest that instead of receiving assistance to grow Fair Trade products, farmers should grow a different crop, or grow high-value crops. This could provide a higher income for farmers, but the climate and ground conditions may not be suitable. It may also be very difficult for farmers to gain the skills and equipment necessary to grow a different type of crop.

 1988 Coffee prices plummet, triggering the birth of the first Fair Trade certification scheme >>>

1994 Coffee, tea and chocolate sell in the UK with the Fair Trade mark for the first time >>>

1998 Third-party certifier of Fair Trade products Transfair USA opens its doors >>>

WHAT THE WORLD THINKS...

These are three publications around the world commenting on the Fair Trade system. Compare and contrast the various viewpoints and see if you can find any more newspaper reports or other media discussing the policy and the alternative CAFE.

Guillermo Vargas Leiton,
Fair Trade website,
2007

'If we didn't have Fairtrade sales, most of the farmers would be cutting down their trees. 100% of our crop is sold to the Fairtrade market. The current price of coffee in the conventional market doesn't cover the cost of producing the coffee...When I think of Fairtrade, I think: Fair for the producer and fair for the consumer.'

Guillermo Vargas Leiton is a coffee farmer in Costa Rica.

***The Economist* website,**
7 November 2006

'[Starbucks] doubts even that the strategy of the Fair Trade movement, to secure farmers a premium over the market price for their beans, is the best basic approach. Starbucks prefers a code known as the CAFE practices (Coffee and Farmer Equity), which aims to help coffee farmers develop sustainable businesses through a mixture of technical support, microfinance loans, and investment in infrastructure and community development where the farmers live.'

***The Japan Times* website,**
23 April 2006

'In Lindsey's [director of the pro-market Cato Institute's Center for Trade Policy Studies] view, if we want to assist coffee growers, we should encourage them either to abandon coffee and produce more profitable crops...or to move into higher-value products, like specialty coffees, that bring higher prices.'

1999–2005 Transfair USA certifies over 33 million kilograms of fair trade coffee, generating US$60 million of additional income for farmers >>> | **2004** Almost £1.50 is spent on Fair Trade goods every second >>> | **2006** Over 1,500 Fair Trade products are on sale in the UK >>>

Anti-globalisation

With every argument for globalisation, there is a contrasting anti-globalisation viewpoint. The way in which globalisation affects democracy, poverty, debt, culture and the environment has been widely criticised in the media. Here we take a closer look at some anti-globalisation arguments.

Decision-making

People who are against globalisation believe that it is eroding democracy. A democracy is a political system in which the general population can participate in decision-making processes. In order to benefit from, for example, IMF loans, the countries' governments must do as instructed. In this way, decision-making is taken out of the hands not only of governments, but also of the general population.

   Global policies and practices are often made by rich and powerful countries, corporations, institutions and individuals. Governments and people in LEDCs are relatively powerless. The LEDCs try to attract investment by reducing wages, reducing the cost of resources and lowering standards. This all contributes to an increase in poverty in the LEDCs.

Debt and poverty

Anti-globalisation supporters believe that debt for LEDCs should be written off. Repaying debt often means that a government cannot provide for the basic needs of its population. The gap between the rich and poor is widening and poverty is increasing as a direct result of globalisation. Here are some staggering facts to highlight this widening gap.

- The richest 10 per cent of adults control 85 per cent of global wealth and 1.1 billion of the world's 6.5 billion population lives on less than US$1 a day.
- The GDP of the poorest 48 nations (one-quarter of the world's countries) is less than the wealth of the world's three richest people combined.
- 1 billion children live in poverty, 640 million live without adequate shelter, 400 million have no access to safe water, 270 million have no access to health services. 10.6 million children died in 2003 before they reached the age of five (or roughly 29,000 children per day).
- 20 per cent of the population in the developed nations consumes 86 per cent of the world's goods.
- The developing world now spends US$13 on debt repayment for every US$1 it receives in grants.
- The richest 50 million people in Europe and North America have the same income as 2.7 billion poor people.
- Debts owed to institutions such as the IMF and World Bank stand at around US$153 billion.

Technology

Most of the wealth generated by new technological inventions stays in the rich countries of the northern hemisphere. Around 97 per cent of patents are taken out in the northern hemisphere. This keeps the technology from filtering down to poor countries in the southern hemisphere.

Culture and terrorism

Globalisation is believed to threaten cultural uniqueness with the world becoming Westernised and local traditions being wiped out. The backlash against this is leading to regional tensions, which are highlighted by the rise of terrorist attacks against the West, such as those in New York in 2001, Madrid in 2004 and London in 2005.

The environment

Environmentalists object to globalisation, and in particular global trade, because of the huge environmental costs involved. Fossil fuels are being used, pollution is produced, habitats are lost and natural resources are being depleted.

> **QUOTE >**
>
> 'Globalization...has done far less to raise the incomes of the world's poorest people than the leaders had hoped...Rather than an unstoppable force for development, globalization now seems more like an economic temptress, promising riches but often not delivering, in the view of many of the leaders at the United Nations conference.'
>
> **Joseph Khan**, *The New York Times*, 2002.

Demonstrators march during an anti-globalisation protest in Brussels in 2001, coinciding with a European Union summit.

Finance

When a country opens its economy, it allows people to invest in the country. For example, someone may guess that the value of a currency will rise. The person then buys some of this currency. If the economy of the country looks unstable, the person sells their investment. In this way, huge amounts of money enter and leave countries very fast, which can devastate a country's economy.

Global campaigns

Some aspects of globalisation have been used to benefit poorer people. Campaigns around the world have recycled mobile phones from MEDCs for use in LEDCs. In parts of Africa, farmers use the phones to access daily fruit and vegetable prices from markets. Some have quadrupled their earnings because they have access to information about potential buyers and prices before making the long journey into towns to sell their produce.

International environmental treaties

International co-operation is attempting to address the environmental issues that are threatening our planet. One of the most famous international environmental treaties is the Kyoto Protocol. This

This woman is talking on her mobile phone to a bank official from the Grameen Bank about the micro-loan program, near Dhaka in Bangladesh. This program grants small loans to poor people who do not qualify for conventional bank loans.

1997 The Kyoto Protocol is drawn up by the UN >>>	2005 The Kyoto Protocol comes into force >>>	2005 China's FDI totalled US$72.4 billion >>>	May 2007 Talks begin on a future treaty that will take over from the Kyoto Protocol when it expires in 2012 >>>

agreement came into force in 2005 and is designed to limit greenhouse gas emissions and prevent climate change.

However, it is difficult for different countries to agree on ways to protect the environment without harming their economies. As a result, some countries did not ratify the Kyoto Protocol, including the USA. The USA suggested alternatives to the agreement. Many countries that did ratify the agreement are struggling to make the changes without harming their economies.

The ozone layer

Global co-operation can benefit the environment. In the 1970s, scientists noticed that the ozone layer was thinning across the globe, especially over Antarctica. They discovered that it was being destroyed by chemicals called chlorofluorocarbons (CFCs), found in aerosol cans, fridges and solvents. In the 1980s, the world's nations decided to do something and, by 1996, CFCs were no longer produced. The ozone layer appears to be gradually repairing itself and some scientists believe that it will be healed in about 50 years.

How China has benefited from globalisation

Since 1978, China has embraced globalisation by opening up its economy to foreign investment. Between 1978 and 2004, its GDP increased from US$147.3 billion to US$1.6494 trillion. Its economy grew each year by 9.4 per cent and its

> QUOTE >
>
> 'There is a chance to make decisions that will lift billions of people out of poverty. Trade can be part of the solution to poverty but at the moment it's part of the problem.'
>
> **Nelson Mandela**, WTO meeting in Hong Kong, December 2005.

foreign trade rose from US$20.6 billion to US$1.1548 trillion. Although poverty is still a big problem, living standards have improved and people are earning more money. But how did China avoid the problems that other countries have experienced with globalisation?

China only allowed foreign direct investment (FDI) when a foreign company went into partnership with a Chinese company. By doing this, a larger percentage of the profits remained within China. This could then be reinvested in China, resulting in a massive growth in China's economy. Additionally, there are not the same intellectual property rights in China. For example, a Chinese company could copy a manufacturing technique used by a MEDC partner company after it has left China. It can use technology and processes that took many years to develop in the MEDC to make its own products. In this way, the MEDC company has trained its competitor.

Case Study: Anti-globalisation protests in Hong Kong, 2005

The sixth Ministerial Conference of the WTO met in Hong Kong between 13 and 18 December 2005. Representatives from 148 countries aimed to reach an agreement about the reduction of subsidies on agricultural products, liberalise farm trade and cut trade barriers across a wide range of other sectors.

Protests

Between 6,000 and 10,000 people arrived in Hong Kong to protest against globalisation and against the WTO in particular. They wanted to influence the

Violent protests by campaigners at the WTO meeting in Hong Kong.

talks to ensure that LEDCs had access to markets in the richest nations – something that current EU and US subsidies prevent. They were angry because they felt that MEDCs were getting a good deal at the expense of LEDCs.

The demonstrations began with a carnival-like atmosphere with protestors carrying huge banners, banging drums and chanting their anti-globalisation slogans. However, violence later broke out. More than 1,000 people were arrested and 175 were injured in the Hong Kong demonstrations. Some media outlets concentrated on reporting the violence, implying that the whole of Hong Kong had turned into a battleground. Other media sources emphasised the fact that only a very small percentage of protestors were involved in the violence. The demonstrators were outnumbered, not by police, but by the thousands of delegates, representative from non-government organisations (NGOs) and journalists attending the meeting.

Export subsidies outcome

The EU agreed to end agricultural export subsidies by 2013 and the USA agreed to end cotton export subsidies in 2006. Although this was hailed as a success by the WTO, many are not convinced.

WHAT THE WORLD THINKS...

These are three publications around the world commenting on the anti-globalisation protests in Hong Kong in 2005. Compare and contrast the various viewpoints and see if you can find any more newspaper reports or other media discussing the demonstration or the outcomes of the WTO meeting.

CNN website, 18 December 2005

'Although demonstrations have largely been peaceful this week, with the exception of a few minor scuffles, the protesters from South Korea escalated their actions on Saturday, attempting to break through a barrier marking the designated protest zone...Police holding riot shields and wearing gas masks tried pepper spray and fire hoses to keep the demonstrators back, then fired tear-gas canisters.'

The Japan Times website, 22 December 2005

'The Battle of Hong Kong was fueled mainly by profound insecurity. Consider the pathos of the South Korean farmers. Hundreds bravely stormed barricades or swam valiantly through Victoria Harbor's waters to try to breach the security barriers around the glamorous convention building hosting the latest WTO meeting. Many hundreds were arrested.'

Australian Broadcasting Corporation (ABC) website, 12 December 2005

'...The protest was the first of a flurry of demonstrations planned over the next few days...Police rate the chances of public disorder as high and say the possibility of terrorist attacks is moderate, although they add there have been no specific threats...'

Chapter 6

Globalisation and the Media

Today's media operates 24 hours a day, seven days a week. Television news channels show constant, rolling stories, daily newspapers are packed with information and the Internet allows us to look up any story or news item at any time of the day or night.

A still showing Sky News's 'eye from the sky' live coverage of the terrorist attacks on London's underground network in July 2005.

Spin and sensation

While good-quality information from media outlets enhances a democracy, poor-quality media can be damaging and dangerous. The mainstream media helps us form our views of the world around us. It influences our opinons and helps us to learn. We can stay informed of events happening almost anywhere in the world.

SKY news 10:48
LIVE
SKYCOPTER

KEEP CLEAR

SKY NEWS BREAKING NEWS
FLASH RAIL UNIONS: ONE EXPLOSIVE DEVICE ON UNDERGROUND

N UNDERGROUND NETWORK HAS BEEN CLOSED DOWN FOLLOWING

However, television channels must fill their air-time. Some people think that because of this, the quality of the information we hear and see is affected. They believe that instead of simply reporting the facts, news outlets make the issues more interesting and gripping. They think that the media may have its own agenda for giving a particular angle to a news story.

Globalisation in the news

Globalisation issues do not always feature in the main news stories. When companies merge, enter a new market or expand, or when international trade agreements are reached, these stories may only be reported in newspapers or the business section at the end of televised news bulletins, rather than in the mainstream news.

However, globalisation does hit the headlines when there are anti-globalisation demonstrations, such as those in Hong Kong in December 2005 (see pages 36–37), Miami in November 2003 and Seattle in April 2000. These clashes can be peaceful or violent and it is possible for the media to take the neutral, anti- or pro-globalisation viewpoint.

Corporate domination

Since the 1980s, there have been a lot of mergers and buyouts in the media industry. So much so that at the start of 2007, there were less than ten media giants dominating the industry (see table right).

There are relatively few independent media outlets because they can't compete with the trans-national corporations (TNCs). But why does this matter? Many people believe that the fewer corporations are in control of the media, the less diversity there is in the types of issues and perspectives that are portayed.

Another of the problems with the media TNCs is that they often control more than one stream of media. For example, Time Warner has interests in television networks, the Internet, magazine publishing, telephone networks and the film industry. People worry about one company having an influence over such a huge variety of media streams.

Top media TNCs

Company	Market value (US$ billion)
General Electric (owner of NBC)	330.93
Microsoft	253.15
Google	147.66
Walt Disney	61.03
News Corporation	57.57
Time Warner	55.83
Vivendi	46.36
Yahoo	37.15
Viacom	25.48

Source: Forbes magazine, 2008

Big business and the media

Many media companies get a large portion of their income from advertising sales. Some people worry that media companies are influenced by those that advertise on them. For example, news stories or articles could be omitted because they may offend the advertising companies.

Advertising also helps to create global brands. The Simpsons, Shell, Xbox, Toyota, GlaxoSmithKline, Kleenex and McDonald's are all global brands, to name but a few. Many people watch between two and eight hours of television each day and advertisments are played between and within most programmes. Some people believe that global brands and advertising spread Westernised culture across the world.

Large companies have many directors who make decisions about how to run the company. Directors of one company may also sit on the board of another company. This is called interlocking directorates. Media companies have directors who are on the boards of pharmaceutical, travel, oil, software, food or security companies. There is therefore the potential for a conflict of interests when it comes to making decisions over what to broadcast.

The Internet – how it is different

The Internet is unregulated and anyone can post information on the thousands of websites that exist. Many people believe that the Internet is a positive part of globalisation that enhances democracy and provides an open forum for discussion

Do you use just a few websites to source all of your news or social information? Are you receiving accurate and diverse information?

Late 1950s Early development of the concept of the Internet begins >>>	1992 The Internet begins to take off as private companies start offering Internet services to the general public >>>	1997 Tens of millions of people are using the Internet >>>

40

Dedicated television channels and websites send information around the world in real-time, enabling traders to constantly buy and sell stocks and shares, as shown here in the New York Stock Exchange.

and trade between people around the world.

Others have their doubts. Principally because anyone can post on the Internet, much of the information is inaccurate or only represents a narrow point of view. Many news outlets buy their news from other companies such as the Associated Press or Reuters. While there is nothing wrong with the news from these sources, it does mean that online news is less diverse than it appears.

Corporations and governments affect the Internet. AOL's website provides users with every type of information imaginable – news, sport, travel, leisure, finance, music, shopping, and so on. In this way, many users just source their information from one site. In some parts of the world, the government sees the Internet as a threat. It attempts to control what is posted online (see running news stream below).

> QUOTE >

'We have no obligation to make history. We have no obligation to make art. We have no obligation to make a statement. To make money is our only objective.'

Michael Eisner, before becoming C.E.O. of The Walt Disney Company.

Real-time information

Today's media provides real-time information to the rest of the world. This means that news and information can travel instantly. This has a big effect on financial markets. If a stock market crashes in one country, the impact travels across the world very rapidly – in 'real-time'.

 2007 1.3 billion people use the Internet worldwide >>> | **2007** 61 [known] people are currently in prison in China for posting online criticism of their government >>> | **2007** The Internet is monitored or controlled in many countries, such as Cuba, Iran, Syria and Tunisia >>>

Case Study: Disney, the global entertainment brand

Disney was founded by Walt Disney in 1923 as a small cartoon studio. Today, it is one of the largest media and entertainment corporations in the world, as well as a global brand. Disney has released more than 270 films, has theme parks in the USA, France, Hong Kong and Tokyo, and owns cable, radio, publishing and Internet businesses.

The Disney brand is instantly recognisable and crosses cultures all over the world.

Childhood memories

Most of us will know Disney from watching animated movies as a child and will recognise the most famous characters, such as Donald Duck and Mickey Mouse.

Disney is known for providing laughter and wholesome family enterntainment. Its cartoons create imaginative, innocent worlds in which usually a hero or heroine battles evil and wins. However, Disney has received a wide range of criticisms including gender, race or class bias.

For instance, women are typically portrayed as a princess, a queen or as someone who works in the home cleaning and cooking. Usually, the women are rescued by a male who is gallant and forceful. People worry about this because fictional characters provide role models for children, and when people are shown in this way it can reinforce gender stereotypes.

Disney corporation

The ABC television network is owned by Disney. Recently, an ABC show called *Good Morning America* gave a lot of air time to a puppet who appears in television adverts for a website called Pets.com. Disney has a 5 per cent stake in Pets.com. In the interview with the puppet, the presenters repeatedly called the puppet by its name – 'Pets.com'. It could be coincidence that the website got some free advertising, but some suspect that Disney saw it as an opportunity to increase awareness of a business in which it holds a stake.

WHAT THE WORLD THINKS...

These are three articles from newspapers around the world commenting on Disney. Compare and contrast the various viewpoints and see if you can find any more newspaper reports or other media discussing the company.

The New York Times, 27 March 2000

'On Feb. 23, the hosts of "Good Morning America", Charles Gibson and Diane Sawyer, were particularly giddy about their guest. The visitor was the comic sock puppet, which looks like a mongrel dog, that has appeared on all the television commercials of Pets.com, an Internet pets-supply company...Go.com, the Internet arm of the Walt Disney Company, ABC's parent company, had bought a stake of roughly 5 percent in the pet site only a month earlier.'

The Times of India, 29 January 2006

'What would childhood be without comic characters? Boring is one word that comes to mind. But thanks to Disney Channel's Disney Magic, some really adorable characters are here to light up our lives...'

The Times, 6 March 2004

'...[B]eneath the cutesy exterior the world that Walt built is a vast money-making conglomerate and home to some of the corporate world's hardest noses...the gritty works of the Disney company are usually hidden from sight, the better to preserve the fantasy...For 70 years Disney has stood as the world's cultural superpower, the supreme arbiter and shaper of childhood imagination...'

Chapter 7

The Future of Globalisation

Globalisation is happening and is here to stay. In south-east Asia, globalisation has boosted growth and lifted millions out of poverty over the last 15 years. China and India are developing at a rapid rate. But the benefits have been uneven and globalisation has, so far, failed the poor in many parts of the world. In sub-Saharan Africa, poverty has worsened, and in many places the gap between the rich and the poor has widened. What of the future?

Globalisation has not affected us all equally. Many people in MEDCs have food, water, shelter and material possessions in abundance (left), but it is a very different story for people in LEDCs (right).

The environment

The benefits of globalisation have been achieved at a huge cost to the environment. Air travel is expected to triple in volume between 1997 and 2015. More jet flights means more burning of fossil fuel, which contributes to global warming and climate change. Indeed, globalisation has so far largely been powered by oil and coal, but fossil fuels are running out. The world must seek alternatives in renewable energy sources, for example sunlight, wind and water, and reduce energy consumption and carbon dioxide emissions.

Is there an answer?

Many people believe that the global community can benefit from a change in globalisation. Critics think that the IMF should be abolished; others say that it needs to be radically transformed. Both sides think that these types of global organisations – the IMF, World Bank and WTO – should become more democratic. By making these organisations more focused on the needs of global citizens, perhaps it is possible to reduce poverty and redress the balance between rich and poor.

Perhaps power should be returned to national governments. An increase in local control may help improve the democracies of the world. Or could new global investment rules stop corporations from making quick profits at the expense of people and our planet?

Globalisation and you

We share our planet and we are all part of the global community. Each of us can have an influence over globalisation by the choices we make in our everyday lives. You could choose your next pair of trainers based on style, price or the conditions of the workers who made them. If you only buy things from your own country, what happens to countries who rely on trade with MEDCs? But if we continue to trade globally, what happens to the environment? How do you think a new type of globalisation can shape a better future for us all?

capitalism Economic system in which products are produced to make a profit. The means for making a product, such as a factory, company or land, are privately owned.

climate change Shift in the world's weather patterns, thought to be brought about by the burning of fossil fuels and subsequent release of greenhouse gases into the atmosphere.

colonisation Control of a country or region by a more powerful country.

culture Beliefs, attitudes and practices shared by a group of people.

debt Money owed by one person, company or country to another.

democracy Political system in which citizens vote to elect who runs the country.

dictatorship Political system in which one unelected person has absolute authority over a country.

economic depression Period in which a country's wealth falls, sales and production reduce and many people are unemployed.

economies of scale The larger a company, the more cheaply it can produce one unit of its product .

economy Wealth and resources of a country.

ecosystem Living things and the environment in which they live.

export Sell something in a different country from that in which it is made.

extinct No longer exists.

FDI Foreign Direct Investment is when a company from one country invests in another country, for example a foreign company could buy all or part of a company in another country, or buy a government-owned firm.

free trade Goods and services sold between countries without any restrictions such as tariffs or quotas.

GDP Gross domestic product is the total value of all goods and services produced in a country, usually in one year.

genocide Deliberate attempt to destroy all people belonging to a particular racial or cultural group.

global brand A particular product or company that is recognised around the world, such as Coca-Cola or Playstation.

global warming Increase in the Earth's temperature thought to be a result of increased carbon dioxide emissions.

greenhouse effect The layer of greenhouse gases in the atmosphere keeping in some of the Sun's heat and making the Earth habitable.

greenhouse gases Gases in the atmosphere that trap heat around the Earth, including carbon dioxide, methane, nitrous oxide, ozone and water vapour.

humanity The quality of being human; the human race.

human rights Certain things that all humans should be entitled to – freedom, justice and equality.

import Buy goods or services from another country.

inflation Increase in prices; fall in value of a unit of currency.

interest Charge applied in return for borrowing money. Interest is usually a percentage of the money borrowed.

intellectual property rights The right to use or make a profit from the creations of another person or company. For example, intellectual property includes inventions, trademarks, trade secrets, and artistic and literary works.

interlocking directorates People placed on the boards of directors of two or more companies that may be in competition.

inventory List or record of stock/goods held by a company.

invest Put money into a financial scheme, company or country, usually with the hope of reaping some reward such as profit.

LEDCs Less Economically Developed Countries are the poorer countries of the world, including the countries of Africa, some Asian countries, Latin America and the Caribbean.

living wage Payment for doing a job that is high enough to allow for a sufficiently comfortable standard of living.

market Economic or geographical area in which products and services are bought and sold.

mechanise Change a process so that it is carried out by machinery instead of by a human or other animal.

MEDCs More Economically Developed Countries are the richer countries of the world, including Europe, North America and Australia.

native Someone living in the place where they were born.

navigation Guidance of something, such as a ship or aeroplane, from one place to another.

ozone layer Layer of ozone gas high in the atmosphere which blocks out a large proportion of the Sun's harmful ultraviolet rays.

patent Document that gives the sole right of a person or company to make, use or sell an invention. Patents usually last for a set period of time and are given out by a government.

privatise Sell a government-owned industry, company or service so that the industry, company or service becomes privately owned.

profit Money gained when something is sold for more than it cost to make, distribute and sell.

protectionism When one country tries to protect an industry from competition by putting up barriers to trade such as imposing tariffs on imports.

ratify Formally approve something such as an agreement so that the agreement can begin to function.

saturated Completely full.

stereotypes Generalised or standardised views of a person or a group of people.

stock market Organised place where professional stockbrokers meet to buy and sell stocks and shares in companies.

structural adjustment Changes to the economic policies of a country, for example the privatisation of government-owned services, imposed by an international body such as the World Bank.

sub-Saharan Africa African countries that are found south of the Sahara Desert.

subsidy Money given by the government to a company, organisation or charity in order to help it function.

surplus More than is needed; an amount left over after requirements have been met.

sustainable Able to be maintained; in environmental terms, sustainable means exploiting natural resources in such a way that the natural balance is not upset.

tariff Money to be paid (tax) on imports or exports, usually imposed by a government.

trade Buy and sell goods and services.

treaty Formal, written and ratified agreement between countries or political groups.

union Group of people with a common interest or purpose, for example employees join worker unions and work together to bargain with the employer for better wages and conditions.

UN The United Nations is an organisation of nations, formed in 1945 to promote peace, security and international co-operation.

war crime Crime committed during war time that goes against international rules of war, for example genocide and mistreating prisoners are both war crimes.

WTO The World Trade Organisation is an international organisation dealing with the rules of trade between nations.

FURTHER INFORMATION >

BOOKS

Global Issues for Secondary Schools: The Challenge of Globalisation (Oxfam Educational, 2007)

In the News: Globalisation by Iris Teichmann (Franklin Watts, 2002)

Just the Facts: Globalisation by Adam Hibbert (Heinemann Library, 2005)

The No-Nonsense Guide to Globalization by Wayne Ellwood (New Internationalist, 2006)

A Very Short Introduction: Globalization by Manfred B Steger (Oxford University Press, 2003)

World Issues: Fair Trade, by Adrian Cooper (Franklin Watts, 2008)

WEBSITES

The Globalisation Guide
www.globalisationguide.org
Answers to key globalisation questions.

Global Education
www.globaleducation.edna.edu.au/globaled/go/cache/offonce/pid/178
Australian website outlining the benefits and problems associated with globalisation.

Project Globalization 101
www.globalization101.org/
Website designed to challenge the reader to look more closely at the controversies surrounding globalisation.

Human Rights Watch
www.hrw.org/advocacy/index.htm
In-depth information on global issues and how they relate to human rights issues.

Environmental Protection Agency
www.epa.gov/climatechange/
US site full of information on climate change – what it is, how it has come about and what we can do about it.

The Fairtrade Foundation
www.fairtrade.org.uk
Free resources, video case studies and recipes.

Walt Disney
www.disneyabctv.com/division/pdf/onesheet.pdf
A list of Disney's wide-ranging media interests.